WIZARDRY

of Love

WIZARDRY

of Love

Bruce Charles Kirrage

Ordering Information:

For orders and inquiries, please contact:
1-888-404-1388
www.goldtouchpress.com
book.orders@goldtouchpress.com

Printed in the United States of America

Dedicated to

AH ML SPD MEB CS PS HBAG WF EJK NQ JD & C DM LNA VH CF MH MJK & A M M-R-D & P MR & A AW & P BW & Daughter & my two sons JPCK & NGK

With special thanks to Norwich Prison, Northgate, BMI Mount Alvernia, & St. Nicholas Church.

Without whom this book would not have been written.

Index

About the Author

Bruce Charles Kirrage was born in Singapore in 1953.

After travelling the world in 1960, he settled permanently in the UK in 1966 and joined the medical profession in 1973, he then retired in 2010.

Mr. Kirrage has been writing poems, prose, and children's stories since 1977. These other writings were also endorsed by a medical consultant.

Mr. Kirrage believes in Christian principles; that God was/is the single entity open to the question of courage, the compassion of human or animal nature, an understanding of happiness, and an interpretation of worldly events.

Other Books:

Wizardry of Women
Wizardry of Man
Burp, Hip, and Twist Children's Book Series

Preface

This book is going to be by far the most challenging to do. On one side it lays bare the vulnerability of this matter and touches upon the childlike innocence of first real love and the other is the confusion and difficulty of dealing with feelings outside of my control.

The health and wealth till death and happiness,
too, dwell in you
One and only me till beyond a tree
As I look down I hear your voice even no sound me spared
The wiser you are by far
You are there whether in or out honour it is… Ta

Honour that will last these favoured isles
Come to the church down
A ridiculous way you have my heart
And everything in it when crying or laughing or speaking out

Loud you are
The crowd that fills my heart
Forever more not a day goes past you are

My beginning, middle, and last

Of Love, Illness, Depression, and Anxiety

'Treated' by medication that can often cause weight gain, as much as thirty percent within three years; it's attributed to a restless leg, body, hand, and arm and/or 'collapsed' thought. Some content of which is perceived as a 'distraction psychosis' people are sometimes mistaken as others. It's concentrated, fast, detailed work, often before sleep.

It's compounded by an inability to relax, with little rest. It's a silent scream of rage within frustration at the inequality in life, in love, and sex. Why? A 'tale' kept between legs and pride. It's being different at worst, calming at best; thinking sometimes forced, sometimes slow, sometimes a little confused, and sometimes very long focused. Crying at something for whatever reason or the utter futility of life over death. At its worst, no cuddle and no kiss from the right woman, moreover assimilation of body/mind together. In its physical imagination, there is all the 'posturing', trying everything, every way possible, in love. It's the lucky 'three' 'four' 'six', 'seven' or 'eleven'; aye, yet it's more than that. The gamut of all this reality will go on and on, day after day, till I eventually die.

For all those having within them to grasp the whole of life's 'cradle of care' are viewed surprisingly and significantly as on 'just another treadmill', for any other reason as 'BAD'. It's said that

I am 'suffered' by others because of 'weaknesses'. It does remain somewhat selfish, or why else would writing be writ.

It's a marriage of suffered years. It's living life in subjugation before, and within. It's interspersed with thought; and throughout by normal behavior which has nothing to do with the situation. I eventually vented my spleen and sent away the ubiquitous 'Snake'; quite a stigma within my quiet thought, that the joke was I, in action abrogates the difference of peace. It's around social nicety a blind reaction, not clever; actually 'uncool', however, for wronged instances.

Further, it's about so little money; no matter, how hard I work! How soon to change! Pah! It's seeing an entity, however, no stowed mind can fathom. It's a 'trunk' call. It's all music. Its love turning and writhing into the circular by my trajectory, yet always attentive to my consort placed first. It's the unremitting reality of the space thereby between; the arc-the flash producing a turn of the wheel, wherein and across the very tiniest part of the brain, a matter to gain ascent. The Pons inside, the ladder to the Pineal, if you wish the key within the lock; nevertheless, on and on past and into a desolate place.

Things change yet intrinsically they are as they have been. The paradox is a race through space yet 'drugged slowly through mud'. It's a statistic measured for early death. It's the cut of love, the very, very, deepest of all. It's no response, yet it is. It's staring into a 'deep black well' which no other term can yet describe. It's a mulch of word, nay; the mind is torn into. It's on waking for a moment not knowing where.

It's time lost, striven to grasp what hour or day. It's finding in a 'bastard' of nature's understanding, of a prime number, of central mood, of an axis of colour, of action, of a disseminated word, and hysterical pain. It's from depression of mind to a dancing euphoria and down to the living surface. It was at the break of dawn a terrifying tangling within. There are tools, weapons seemingly to conjoin to fight during this torment of a tear with medicine; its taking patience, courage, and compassion now with laundered understanding, an interpretation, a right word, - of hand and to mouth

Brian and Marmaduke

For varicose reasons, Brian was not happy; his favourite football team Rottenham Hotspur had been beaten 17 - 0 by Leicester Spastics; he had just recovered from Lumbosis. Brian was sure he could feel an attack of Thrombago coming on, and Marmaduke's girlfriend, Montmorency, hadn't turned up for their date either.

But the thing that disturbed him most of all was the Afrogeisha Question. Only the day before he had heard Mr. Cameron uses a sanctuary against Afro geisha; after all, it was time the Wag(s) had home rule or something.

He knew all about the 'State of Affairs' in African countries; had read all about Homo Kenyatta and the Mew Mew. Heard the news about Highly Selassie and the Seminal question, been in the thick of it when Lumbomumbojumbo, Kasa Booboo and Shombee had caused all that rumble in the Bongo; knew all the leading African politicians; Kennel Kaunda, Nrumour and his rival Leading Seamen Admiral Open wide, Perfecto Fair wood, and lately Chou-En-Odinga, The Grand Pyramid of Egypt and his sisters, 'The Jinx'; Ian Myth, Doctor Nob-in-Y ear-Eary(An old howler), the Grand Poo F. of Katrina and The Waves, and a sea-dog called Olawole Abeagdo.

He decides to drown his sorrow in music.

Not being able to choose between 'Stranger on the Shore' by Acker Bilk and Moriarty's Buffoon Concerto, he settled for a hot piece of lagywotnot by his favourite group, Ravish and

Shankher. Brian resolved to sitar down and let the music flow over him like the stinking water of the Misappropriate Misery River. Marmaduke stood around and looked on.

Now there was another question to be answered for the Incumbent - the American Problem.

It was known that on at least one balmy moonlit night he had beamed a smile from 'ear to ear'.

The Resident before him seemed to have done the wrong thing - he had stepped up the war against the CluelessClan by forming the Do-Re-Me Boys; had fought and lost against Ho-Chi-Chin; and now the V.C. were dropping from hairy planes using a bamboo shoot, handing out ball-joint pens inscribed with the Immoral Words 'Long live Mao-Tse-Dung and the Glorious Pheasants Retribution'.

He certainly had devised a problem to work on, considering he imported such eccentricities as sitars, guitars, cigars, Havana Bananas and a Phothpah of a Prussian Inter-Constipational Plastic Rissole by way of Japan. However, he had lasted this far. He did know though that his 'time' was nearly up.

Marmaduke and Brian whereupon leaped to their feet (presumably because they were trying to escape) smashed Ravish and Shankher into a million pieces and jumped down the stair screaming a fearless 'Banzai!'

(Irish for the gob is rough but the breath is well-oiled) waiving the banner of all their favourite organizations - The C.N.D. (Chronic Neurotic Diastrophic), Lateral/ Laderal, Ladder wrist, and Manicurist. A walking, talking, 'Pollock-Box' of society. Then ... There was/is Donald Trump

King Pantah (A docu-fiction)

This is the story of King Pantah who was nick-named Quad because he was one of the first quadruplet babies that were born around the time of the Celts and the impending invasion of Britain by the Romans.

Quad can be described as huge, with the look of an owl, a long beak for a nose, elongated pointed ears, similar to those of Dr. Spock in Star Trek. He stood about 240cm tall, wore sandals and weighed 150kg.

An emotional character that throughout the previous six months had waged a long-standing feud against King Royale known locally as the killer.

Killer was a Mandingo (of mixed blood) and built quite differently to Quad. He resembled a brick wall. He was bald. His head shaped like a bullet. He wore the equivalent of twenty-inch collar shirts and his biceps were as thick as the thigh of any man. He did not walk. He ambled along an upright gorilla. As both, their armies arranged to meet each one. This outcome was by now much weakened. They each had other for a duel, very early at sparrows' minus to decide the matter.

Quad had requested a wrestling bout between them earlier. A few days had passed and the appointed time had now arrived. On entering, Quad shouted something about the world is a mad place and everyone, including the 'killer', was all insane. At these unusual, unwelcome remarks King Royale quickly strode over and gave the other a hefty shove, nearly flattening him against the wall. Quad immediately saw 'red' and flew at the 'killer', with fists flailing; however, this sudden angry response gave him no advantage.

King Royale just stood on his toes and grabbed Quad in a vice-like head-lock with his opponent's neck and back bent forwards and his face looking directly at the floor. Quad soon began to weaken as bits of his teeth were now breaking up under the increasing pressure. He was forced to tap King Royale near his left kidney with his right hand as a sign of his submission. He had quickly realized just before that if this fight went any further his neck would be broken and that would be his end. He was released. He had already become unconscious and Quad slowly slid to the floor. Although eventually, he was able to get up, muttering something about the Saviour of All Souls. He hesitantly and unsteadily made his way back to his headquarters to recuperate from his ordeal.

Later they were able to meet again and this time apologised to each other. Peace had at last returned. For over a week longer Quad had been suffering from pain and his head was crook. So a colleague was asked if he could help. He stood behind, one fist placed against his upper back, while Quad was seated, and firmly snapped back his head with the other hand, and with a loud, sharp crack his head, neck and vertebrae had finally fallen into line.

Long before this fight ever commenced, Quad was camped in the South and his men were in strict training. Unknown to him he was dealt a devilish trick by a man named Misery, renowned for awkward, indolent behaviour, who had a sad, forlorn expression always written all over his face.

During the long summer months, things were getting worse and food was becoming scarce. One time, during breakfast Quad sensed that all was not well with him. He slowly moved over to the tea urn while trying to make sense of what was going on. At the back of his confused mind, he guessed that his reaction must be due to some drug or other. How had he ingested them? His illogical mind jumped to conclusions and told him two things. He had been tricked and someone had put something in his tea. Although underneath he knew he had no real proof. However, there was no mistaking the mood he was in.

He was very angry.

He further reasoned that Misery may have gone to a Witch Doctor for a grain of a strange compound near the Kings Town. He had been informed that Misery was involved in knife fights with local gangs who were marauding the area. These two disturbing ideas were running side by side through his brain. His feelings quickly escalated into action. He strode across the room and punched the taller, older and stronger Misery on the chin.

He was immediately set upon by about six of the others, beaten up and formally taken to a local hospital. While there he was subjected to many injections, electric shocks, and all manner of fiendish potions were administered.

Throughout that era of his horror, fear and suffering there occasionally came into his mind strange words as if from far away. The weight of any truth hung limply about his shoulders. Through his eyes and ears he imagined the sights and sounds of many years ago as he remembered those childhood years and from within he produced a small whimper at first but this quickly escalated into a loud cry, straight from the heart.

Many months previous as he was lying, somewhat stupified, sprawled on his hospital bed, thoughts and sounds again manifested themselves to him arising from broad open moors. Suddenly he was moved to say "One who has seen all but is yet not seen". King Pantah began to laugh at other thoughts and of lyrical paraphrases. He turned to Robert who was sitting nearby and began to say "Now listen here there's going to be a...." and then suddenly stopped because nearby sat John who was consumed by intense giggling and contagious laughter. He was looking strange like someone from a Billy Bunter cartoon caption.

King Pantah soon began to write down things as he groggily peered through the fog of his potions writing with taut and merry-making but with the truth that he was forty years old having lost a young sweetheart somewhere. Will he stay small in stature and bearing while all around me there are sounds of coughs, sneezes, and wheezes of smokers and passive sleepers? Soon the air around began to be ever so slightly rendered, torn apart by small hacking coughs trying to hide occasional embarrassing noises as if from an old buffalo which was for a few lingering moments surreptitiously letting off underwater while bathing in a lake or stream.

Meanwhile, he mused over these matters with his last remaining thoughts now of how time was passing so slowly. He glanced at the contrasting digits against the face of his watch as he slipped away into a deep sleep. He began dreaming, counting the days until he would see the analog sun-dial.

Finally, he was released and journeyed far away to begin a long rest. However, that did not stop him from forming another fearsome army while residing there. It was not long before he was again brought bad news. The Romans were soon to land at Dover and in large numbers.

He quickly collected his men together and told them they must now march south. He arrived at the Cliffs of Dover and saw several Roman boats about to land nearby. He jumped off the cliffs and plummeted downwards. Then suddenly he opened both legs very wide. His right foot went crashing through one boat, and his left through the other.

The other Romans who were in the ships moored not very far away were so amazed and startled by this feat by Quad that they very soon began to laugh. They laughed almost too much. So that it had begun to hurt and were unable to fight properly. At last, they decided that the best course of action was to retreat so they could perhaps come back and fight another day.

Quad was very fortunate; he had only suffered minor flesh wounds. He had not broken any bones despite his long fall. However, his body ached for many days and he had some difficulty walking, but secretly very proud and relieved that he had survived.

Now the church in Rome was gaining a lot more power and its rulers had established ever greater influence, almost as much as his own kingdom, yet not quite. Quad had been decorated with colourful medals which he was obliged to always wear. Emissaries carrying gifts for him were sent from Rome and elsewhere. He was unable to shy away from the pomp and ceremony. He was an ancient celebrity. People visited him in their thousands and he dutifully tried to thank as many as possible. A coin was struck to mark the occasion and had been inscribed with both his name and pseudonym as Quad.

Afterward, the Times hit the streets with the headline carved out on a large silican stone tablet 'Quad stamps on four galleons!'

It was announced that he should be given the lion's share. Many coins were given to King Pantah or Quad as he was affectionately known and his popularity quickly grew. For a long time, everyone lived happily and those unusual coins were generously given to him by people.

Guilt and Worry

Guilt usually indicates worry;
if there is no guilt, then there is no worry.
However, it's not all plain sailing or as simple;
worry causes 'immobility', it does not always imply guilt.
There is always room to give the benefit of the doubt, -
that's called civilization; although how civilized are we?

Be (a little) wary of the words hope, wish and maybe.

Do not do tomorrow what I can do today,
but think of it as a process and a way forward.

Essentially, you are an external type of person if you assign
responsibility for your emotional state to someone else or
something external.

If you are asked: 'Why do you feel bad?' Your reply
'My parents mistreat me' or 'My luck is down',
then you are in this external category. Most are.

If you are asked: 'Why do you feel bad?' Your reply 'I tell myself
the wrong things' or 'I worry about what others think about
me'; rare in our culture.

However, if one is of the above by nature,
it's found hard to suffer without an opinion or bias.
Most of us are one or other at certain times. 'Gut Instinct'

(sex and logic) = Belief+ Bias. 'You are being yourself etc.
[Syllogism: Aristotle].

You are muster bating when you find yourself behaving in ways
that you feel you must, even though you (might) prefer some
other form of behavior (OCD).

Facts+ reason= consideration+ action=
consequence and resolution

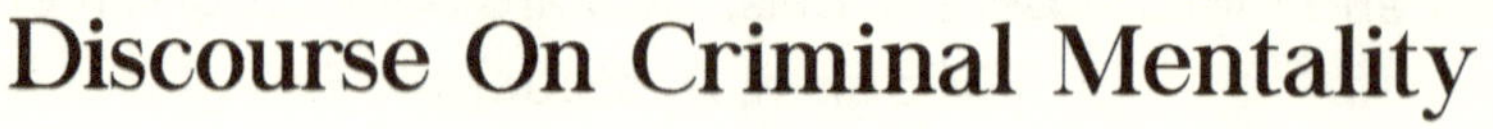

Discourse On Criminal Mentality

Extracts from The Criminal Mentality by John Bartlow Martin:

'He wanted to become famous'. Shocking, spectacular, and seemingly senseless crimes make us wonder whether a 'Criminal Mentality' or 'Killer Instinct' exists. Maybe well to dispose of the notion that man is a peaceable animal... one remembers Auschwitz... modern terrorist activity.

Of all the carnivores - only two lack built-in inhibitions against killing members of their species - rats and men.

What shocks us most of all is a murder 'without reason'... most of all... mass murder.

People can accept the idea that lunatics kill (actually they seldom do).

They simply do not have the wherewithal.

Of all the factor involved in criminality, the most important is the subtle relationship between members of the family... this is far closer to psychiatry or psychology than sociology.

It is no exaggeration to say that the administration of criminal justice is the best measure of any society. (This is because it is self-apparent when correctly applied).

We must sift out the strands of thought and conclusions reached by their book. True, there are many inconsistencies in the prison and hospital model, (not least one of repetitive 'sick' or 'criminal' behaviour), however, to my mind every person needs to try and resolve his or her own conflict (mental and physical) by their belief to improve and develop. This can be summed up by perceiving an "extension" of our own reality to tap into our own understanding or interpretation, compassion, and courage. Notwithstanding the fact that everyone's reality is often very different, however, it's in the belief or perception in the common 'extension' of that which does matter. For all of us, it's much more of a moral choice than anything else thereby creating a dependence on those virtues.

There a few small questions:

Are all rats 'Killer or King Rats?'

During the 2nd World War Germany picked out these 'types' of prisoners and sent them off to places where they were essentially under closer guard which was Colditz.

The ratio was approximately 1:20

A psychiatrist treated a bloke for 3 years unsuccessfully as he claimed he was always on the outside looking in, that was until he found out he was a window-cleaner.

This simple tale exemplifies the ideas of perception understanding and interpretation which can help to find the fundamental key.

Man was given two ears and one month; the reason being he was supposed to hear more and speak less. (Buddha 2500 years ago)

Two things to worry about - either you are well or you are sick. If you are well - fine, if you are sick then there are two things to worry about - either you will get well or you will die.

If you get well there is nothing to worry about.

If you die there are only two things to worry about - either you go to heaven or hell; if you go to heaven - congratulations, if you 'go to hell' - a joke.

'I would love to have the ability and/or wisdom to upset lesser and improve moreover'.

TAO Principle (Looking Eastward)

Stretch (visualize anima/one's own woman/child; always fit)

Simplify (visualize Nash/Einstein/Pope)

Follow and lead your hopes and dream

Who laughs, laughs (best) because he has thought of a contrite interpretation.

Humour is by far the most significant activity of the human brain. (Edward De Bono)

Jokes

Spinach certainly has a lot of iron in it.

Popeye coughed and nailed Olive Oyl to the wall!

"Listen hard. Speak soft. 'See' well. Give .... 0.7 % to charity...?

A man visits his doctor complaining of back pain due to a cricket ball stuck there. 'How's that? The doctor commented. To which the man replied 'Oh no, not you as well'.

Note to ponder: The American Journal of Urology calls itself 'The Official Organ' of the American Urological Society.

A man enters a pub, tells everyone 'I'm 62 today'. They all buy him a drink. As he got up to leave he turns to everybody and comments 'I'm 62 today and tomorrow 2 till 1 O'.

An Irishman thought Hertz-van-Rental was a Dutch footballer.

Man, 73, marries a girl 23, goes to his doctor for some advice. The doctor says that perhaps a good idea would be to get a lodger. The man replies 'Of course, I'll do that'.
A few months later he meets the doctor again and the doctor asks after the wife. 'Oh, she's OK' and again after the lodger 'Oh, she's expecting too!'

Last week, according to the Financial Times the £ closed at 69 cents to the Used Ugandan Tissue.

An old film used to be called "Callaghan and the No Chance Kid" or 'Rags to Riches tale'

What's the difference between a rat lying in the road and a banker? The rat has skid marks around it!

Riddles in Puddles

Why are computers like houses? - Because they have windows.

Do robots have brothers? - No, only transistors.

What's worse than raining cats and dogs? - Hailing taxis.

What's the difference between a 'Crack Den' and a Jehovah's Witness/ Mormon? You can shut the door on a 'Crack Den'.

What's the difference between a seagull and a new-born pup? A seagull flits all over the shore.

What's the difference between a goldfish and a mountain goat? A goldfish mucks about in mountains.

Why is a girl's belly-button like a yard light? Because it's half-way between the milk-house and the tool shed.

Laying the table is a good way to get yourself a drink. (American style)

A young doctor was very worried by all the young girls visiting his surgery for pregnancy tests. He mentions this to an older colleague. 'There seems to be something in the air at this time of year - can you tell me what it is?'
'Their legs' the other replied, drily.

A Labour girl and a Tory Backbencher were very much in love and eventually married. On their first night, instead of mad passion, they ended up in a double-bed with their backs to one another because of a silly quarrel about politics. After about twenty minutes the girl said in a rather timid voice 'Darling, there's been a split in the Coalition Party and if the Tory stood now he would easily get in.' 'Too damn late!' he retorted. 'He's stood as an Independent and lost his deposit! However, I am an 'early riser' so we'll pass an act to reinstate this thing tomorrow morning!'

A pretty young nun on her first day at the convent meets the priest for her interview. He explains to her that under his habit he has a key which will fit her lock and she will then be able to go to heaven. She believes him and he has his way with her. Afterwards she is very happy, gets dressed, runs off to Sister Superior to tell her all about it, including the explanation about the lock, the key and that she will now definitely go to heaven. On hearing the young nun's story, Sister Superior is indignant and explained that she had been told the same story and asked to blow on Jacob's Horn too. That was more than twenty years ago, and she still hadn't gone to heaven!

An animal. Horne Alone. 'Leopard'

Indecent. When it's long and hard then it's in decent.
(Promote calming from heaven)

Impotence. Emission Impossible. (Need courage dear)
Aphrodisiac. Money (aka Food and Wine)

Navajo Erection. Scrotum Pole (Work and women)

Seduction. The art of genital persuasion
(does put lead in your pencil)

Polysaturated. Pissed parrot. (Equality)

Smallest bikini. Two bands and a cork.
(Irish Uprising) Drizzle. Drip that's going steady. (Peace at last)

Mons Venires. Fanny Hill. (Come to me o'er yonder mountain)
Roman house flyer - Titus Andronicus

Boy and girl anxious to make love in the park which was
closed. Tried to climb the high wall to try and get in
unsuccessfully. 'I have an idea' said the boy fumbling with his
flies. Here, stand on this. 'Great' retorted the girl. 'But how do
we get to return?' he asked. The girl's immediate reply to this
seemingly difficult question was 'Didn't you know I was an ex-
Russian Pole Vaulter? We can easily return in the morning'.

A Christian can have sixteen wives:

better

worse

richer

poorer

To diagnose a 'Gonorrhea' insert staff into Virginia and listen
out for the slow clappers.

Why is a lady's leg like a cheque? When it's crossed they're
safe, however when open it has a certain advantage.

The difference between being hard up and down and out is
around one's minuets'

Did you hear of the bloke who had a bald head and a lot of
rabbit tattooed on his scalp.
From a distance he looked like a dog.

A man enters a pub with a crocodile under his arm and
asks the barman if he serves Bastards here. 'Of course, we
do, sir' 'Good, I'll have a double-whiskey and a Bastard for
him'. Around 10 p.m. he orders another and another and
another, all of the same. Eventually, the barman says that now,
unfortunately, they have completely run out of Bastards and
would chocolate do. They have some kept out the back of the
pub. To which the man replies 'What! Start him on 'Little Phi
squares' at this time of night'.

Then there was the story of the woman who sued Sainsbury's
for forging her tattoo on their Hot-Cross Buns.

An agent went with his young rising star to see a producer
and exclaimed. 'This fellow is brilliant; he is able to speak out
the back of his rear!' 'Alright, let's see him perform' said the
producer. Whereupon the young actor stood in the middle of
the room and promptly shat all over the beautiful, expensive,
white carpet; the producer was incensed and yelled out
'What's with this guy, he's ruined my carpet!' To which the
young man replied 'I'm very sorry, sir, I was just clearing my
throat'.

If a light sleeper sleeps with the right one,
does a hard sleeper sleep with a wrong 'un?
Does a Rubber neck sleep with a rubber on?
'What do virgins dream of?'
'I don't know.'
'I thought you didn't'.

Johnny Cradock, overheard on a radio show,
"And you too can have a ring like Fannies!"
Dyslexia rules........KO Logic rules OK
Amnesia rules......Er, Um, Er, Um, Er
'Mother, my boyfriend's a monk; he's got a dirty habit.
'We'11 soon break that!'
Or
'Mother, my boyfriend's an Atheist;
he doesn't believe in hell'.
Or
I proposed to a girl while recovering.
I said I was an Agnostic,
However I was sure; or
'Mother, my boyfriend's a writer;
he doesn't talk to me about his work'
'Marry him'.

'Do you like kissing? 'You can kiss the car goodbye,
I've just wrecked it'

What succeeds Budgies with no beak?
Thought naught of it.

Two Irish fellows in court.
Judge asks "Where do you live?"
First reply "No fixed abode, sir" Second replies
"The flat above him"

A man, heavily disguised, goes into a chemist and whispers,
'Can I have a packet of cheap Tampax please?'
'Why?'
'I want to be able to ride my bike to work in comfort (Ugh)

Welshman: All the English are either cricketers or prostitutes.

Scotsman: My mother and father were English Welshman:
What position did they play?
Scotsman: 'Bowler and Man at Third leg'

Famous Australian choir with orchestral composition but no
vocals 'Roll over Sheila'.

Irish builder come over from Dublin, has a few beers on his
first evening. Following day, feels a bit wobbly, falls off the
building he was working on - Thud! Very soon after he hits the
ground an old lady sees him; she rushes over and asks, 'What
happened?' Irishman replies 'I dunno, just got here?!'

'How many times does a plane crash?
........On average?'..... 'One'

Bad news: 'We cut off your legs and transplanted two ballet
dancers' legs; grafted locks from a Taft in Wales over your
bald 'Oh, what's the good news?'...patch, changed the colour
of your skin, and replaced your own with that from a Flemish
carpet salesman'.

'Well... You're top of the Council Housing list!'

Have you heard the one about the old Irish Wartime golfer
who went out in 39 and back in 45?
Psychiatrist to batty old spinster who has been placed under
his care because of her unsocial behavior 'Can you 'Free-
Associate' now madam?' To which the old lady replies 'Don't
be filthy, young man, I'm over 80 years old, and anyway I don't
believe in sex before marriage!'

Man confesses to a doctor saying that he has been harboring
an illegal immigrant in his cellar and charging him an exorbitant

rent. The priest affirms that this is OK and attempts to placate the man. 'But he's been there 22 years and I haven't explained to him about the Amnesty!'

With his wife dressed in her negligee and on their wedding night the husband asks if he can have a bath. Her reply is affirmative. He gets into the bath and then commands her to, 'make waves...and pull the light cord on and off quickly'... meanwhile he starts kicking the bath noisily with his feet. With this entire rumpus going on the wife is beginning to get desperate and asks him whether he wants to have sex!

Scotsman,
Englishman and Irishman before German Firing squad.
To present a distraction the Scotsman shouts 'Hurricane' all runs for cover and the Scotsman escapes. The Englishman plays a similar trick and he too escapes. However the Irishman stands there spits and yells 'Fire, fire, fire'.

A woman is found wandering around the jungle, apparently lost. Someone asks her 'What's the matter?' To which the woman replies 'Just had an encounter with Lawson and I've "lost all my 'earrings!"

Chicken goes into a library and asks for a book and promptly goes out with it under his arm. Next day same thing happens. And the next, and the next. But he never returns the books. Meanwhile the librarian is getting a bit worried by this rather odd behaviour and he decides to follow the chicken. They both travel far out into the country where there is a large pond and sitting in this large pond on a leaf is a frog. The chicken keeps throwing the books at him whereupon the frog discards each and every one while he croaks 'red it... red it... red it'...

Dalai Lama enters Pizza Express and places his order 'Make me one with everything with spherical objects thrown in'.

A driver in his XJ6 is tanking down the motorway at about 85 when a Cooper flies past with sparks shooting out the back. Cheeky little sod, thinks the Jaguar owner, I've got to have one of those, so he struggles to keep up with the mini. Eventually the mini turns off into a service station. The man runs over to the owner of the smaller car and exclaims 'Just name your price and I'll buy your car'. To which came the reply 'the answers NO'. The Jaguar driver is a bit taken aback by this and asks 'I'm a bit puzzled, what were all those sparks flying out the back of your BMW, I couldn't fail to notice? To which came the reply 'Sod it! My sister left the hand-brake on again.

Logical Postulation

a (alive, of thinking)
b I exist (existence, of work\rest\play)
c I live (a 'humgum' with sections of blasts of humour)
d In hope\zest (refer to a)
Free will cannot be augmented or changed in any way and may
be by the study of physics as to confer that very small particles
can be observed by 'Luck' or the throw.
'Dice of God'

Coincidences:

Something happening in the same place, however different,
though at identical moments in time. I thought with or without
physicality.' Happenings' currently in two separate places.

My belief this is the mechanism of 'love' i.e. 'insight' and
'outsight'. The next clue deduced from the phrase 'Ma. he's
making eyes at me'. This is foremost when both faces relax into
a smile of understanding, compassion, and wonder'.

Moreover, has no truth other than within own narrative\
innocence. The paradox: 'The power is with woman, not
man.' The source is within her own energy. Therein you have:
Einstein's Theory is one analogous to love i.e. $E = MC2$.

Energy = Woman = Mass (man) x belief/hope/ethic
(speed of light or accelerometer)

Was this also R D Laing's reality when he wrote
'The Divided Self an assertion that there is no mental illness.
I simply referring to the 'book's title'.

For me a 'simple division does not equal an equation on both
sides. Life is much more than that. Thereby the balance is
therefore 'not struck yet demonstrable'.

However, Math proofs explain otherwise.

A particle is 'Energy's' derivative;

Element: with its own characteristic;

A mother's derivative is 'The Psyche-apparent'.

Feedback - neural connection with a parcel of stability likely 'a
pain' or 'a pleasure'.

Wisdom (see definition)* may be drawn from this. To 'secure
happiness within' 'tis everyone's desire, surely; compassion
in understanding and courage in the face of our enemy
which is more so without within ourselves - hate, fear, cruelty,
jealousy etc.

*Wisdom - Reflection, the noblest; imitation, the easiest; and
experience, the bitterest of cheer.

The six attributes of democracy can include the Government
the Judicial and the Monarchy which may be properly brought
alive by the attainment throughout by adding
'Truth, Justice and Goodness'.

Within all our vision and hope an aim. All for one and one for all; a sort of 'Kindly Unity'.

Very many close physical diverse neural connections are needed enabling good spurious humour amid very short cross-synapse time lapses.

All psychiatric medicines counteract and change this basic instinct in some way.

Love does break through this 'barrage' of medication.

Neural synapse 'dissociation' is a catastrophe.

Humanism can lend itself to upper, middle and lower case.

Animus Anima Animal

Id Ego Super-Ego

Animal Vegetable Mineral

Paper beat stone

Stone beat scissor

Scissor beat paper

Quotes

Your face is a book,
where men may read strange wonder and matter

(Attributable to the Tempest, Act 1 Scene 2)....

'This above all:

To thine own self be true

And it must follow

As the night the day

Thou canst not then be false to any man'
'Admit impediments

Love is not love when it alteration finds' as we are
'An open jar, no one is God.

All we really have here is belief, music, wit,
a smile and laughter'.

Possible, though somewhat naive ways to try and solve the
Iraq, Afghan, Syrian, and Iraq/Iran wars and their problems:

Take all possible means to reduce extreme religious and/or
ideological beliefs and actions.

Jaw, jaw. Not war, war

Replace the cash crops of say
Heroin with Saffron Utilise Casava.

Actively promote trade

May lead to a better redistribution of
power and ensuing survival.

Walk away from trouble

Pound up and the value of interest will be down

Pound down and the value of interest will go up

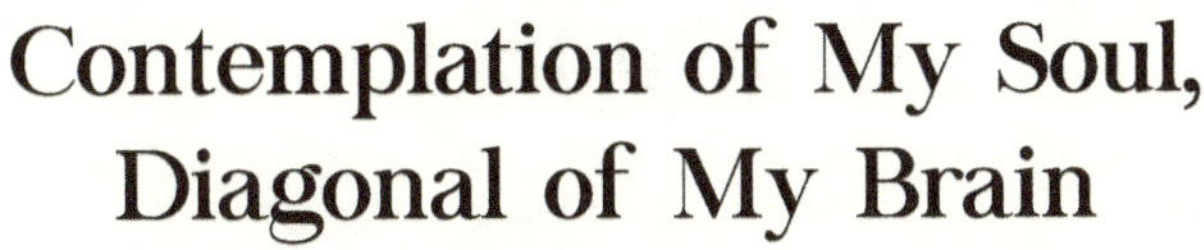

Contemplation of My Soul,
Diagonal of My Brain

Not till her coming through my door with a coat will I know
what I have said. For twenty years now and more I have lived
a proud, honest and trustworthy man - nothing do I miss yet.
Now in a cradle nursed by others will much later die a quiet
death, 'Le petit mart' once and again and gain.

The Tory PM can it also be as if for ten year -
no, unbelievable at this moment.

2016 - She will ask of me this time. My gift is my love and I cry.

I cry for her. Her pain is mine.

What is this riddle? What am I really to be? What do I scream?
Strong in mind D did say. I had to agree. A Shakespeare
reel with which to fish. I have an old rod of about five feet
now down to two foot six. And an extra rod of twelve feet
coupled with a Shakespeare. A computer left to haggle with, a
computer or four a mouse in a drawer and room to breathe.

Drawn to You

Wherefore am I then?

Are you here with me till time knows when?

What else to ask for?

As a Spiritualist I am asked by a widow of three.

My ' old man' I believe watches over, a crane at his feet and a gourd to offer with a light bulb on at his head, tilted and big.

'A gap filled by I write as fit to spit!

Blow all this shit!'

'Blow in the eye, cold dark sky'

'Dressed in braces, yes was crazes'

'Tighten as whiten, out of sight' and

'Drum as sound, come around'

'Beasts cream "' this gorging dream'

'Finger tighten, so enlighten

'Sunk as a ship, let's give it rip'

'Drawn as tight now is my chord is my sword'

And the swirling, stirring, curling, edgy woman comes hard
I know this as she blows crows and does for me as no other
Time and place are changed and reflection rearranged And I
think myself lucky

To have been 'ere so plucky in dealing with the mucky Side
of all

And yet

The knowledge that was and is I will never forget

How she won my heart Never

Never as yet Byrne

A complete confounding woman

A just picture of the science of art

If I were Les and her Liza

Instead I as mad B

And only as wish for a truce how I can always

So that forever pleases her

"A Spider"

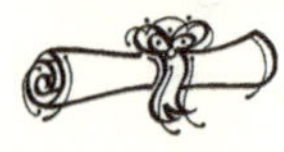

Once some age ago a spider

Did to rest to alight on my board

Now is hanging in its own space

Calm and quiet

Now it is heading upwards

To my ceiling, its seeming desire

Now has come down and alighted

On a floor and gone away

The Venusian

As she can and does;
There only one that puts cream in my
Americano and chins in my chin-ups
A balmier night was never had before when a true Venus came
to me along a walkway out of the blackness of nothing and to
the whiteness of everything behind her dress
Carrying the spunky tones to me of the shootings of zebra and
a doubling of my single prime as 'I run up her ladder';
Give me your love I will plea and I yours
(and a good heart and better action)
For one bucketful of her, the men would trade the world,
One ounce of knowing her compassion and to her my oodles
of my understanding,
For an interpretation of with loving
A plethora of me giving

Fishing a Day in July

The fish come biting and I

Sit and wonder at it

Firstly arrives one here

A small dear

That is one and then another

For soon there is

A monster the only one

Hits speed at a ton

The line hook rod broke

My head in a yoke Lost gone

Say good folk Text you all 'do aye'

Ok with you aye

Yet defy

Everything and everyone

Why

Effing crazy at #M/the shrink at one Tablets/injection/thinking
Poetry/house/homing Normality singing heart

Thou are thou art

Yes back to you

Now you r u 2

Moving you moving you

England

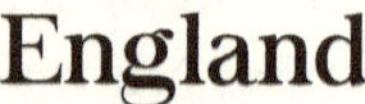

Forever fuel Horse before cart

The England and for Dingo land

Dot I the cross a T

MPs and Cues someone were Sue

A cross till time asks the way

The Mrs. EB and of course

There was May

Don't ask The Why

Say Yes for Essex and Aye

Cream in my coffee Black Beauty

A queen remaining unseen

To a-marryin'

Carry-in too in a bairn

SAS sassy

Seal heal

Sick Dick

C For Three

Forty two

Give it to me you

Give me worth you and you

How I ache the pen to leak

Then hear me/it

Speak

Keep it

Grace by God I'll blow

The shite

As I

Hit that height

Chinaman

A cat named Blue

And AZ to flog that dog

Squeeze the cog to grow

Sow my bones

Away with cones

Stir my tomes

Groans under the udder and ladder weight

Krait snake has nothing for it

Spate out black lout

Black or White

Too few Sew

Mew

Grew back gong tong to which

We hold Vee of new and yeah bold

Cold harbour fish for

'Ardour as harder'

Softer now as I relax Cow and Gate spilling

My slate my lust

Flick to Dick it

Done dusted

Then over and over never

Never it be said

Clever

Now to finish

Trick

Now diminished relaxed

Beaten and by egg and two

Tested the black within the white

Flustered

Yes for a long delay

Black looking black slacks relaxes

And always the Goddess lifts up what

Does with whacks waxes

All There Whiles

All there whiles Hopeful smiles

Across the moors

Lives the girl

With her hair to unfurl

Across the miles

To free her

I know I ought to

Put me to task

Is all I ask?

As a young boy I did sought and

'Stirred'

Give me to her done

Baby-god and lonely

The real one

Comes and goes

Ebbs and yet flows

One and to us as one

For you know and see me

In my mind

In my voice as I talk write do

Let's walk the walk

Be you be for me do yet glue

Intonation Of

Lacking Sleep

Was near weep

And without I wait

Ever hopeful crammed back

The suckling balls in their sack

Look to you more

Gap after this lull

When considered as now yet barely free

Those balls convincingly

Head up

Let CAREFULLY loose upon thee

The drugs and my woes

From my head to my toes

Lesser thence hence

You may ask 2017

Your to me with THENCE and

An aspect of my affection

Will be the right

Direction

Live happily ever after

Us You See

The Attitude

Fishing for you

Why so I do

God is played

Forever is swayed

To yes or we

And others be

The gist in all of us

Thus think the right words

Coursing with all swords

Yet love her madly more

More than forever awe

And I cry with the suffering

And wishing time itself on in

Could remonstrate within

The remorseless finding

A unitary kindling

Could be more or less

Done With PP

This is

Explain X

M word emphasis

Come away from Monday to Sunny day

What is?

Left to two is

God is this

Much for I

It is

Z for zizz

Sleep where that

Spat spit pay

Every day

Marriage

If that were everything

I would bring you to me

If that were you be

My heart is ours

This thing of love is far out to the border less

Bring me love

Hasten yes

Hell to Heaven

Hell is a space that allows a wandering

Hell to heaven

One house to home this

Hell is where the house you own is

Hell is two more beside

Not died

Heaven is hope in there the dream

AS IF

To seem

Hell is when I stuff my pockets

Fain does as if pill with pride

Heaven is about what is to be and could be done

Heaven is eating food cooked

And enjoyed by one

And even to all

Heaven is with hope the sea

To stretch on

Hell is thinking too much

About what you think such

And not about as they blink

Heaven is thinking and the thought

Of now knowing her

Once as if forever too true

Heaven is to know that

Just a little Yes

Just a sprocket within

To dock

Of here remembrance is

Of me and of you

You and me

I and you

She/you/me/they is in there and therein

Around me yet move to yet

Be still

And I feel and as only me as if wondrous fool

And can see in imagining us three too

A Delicate Line to Be Drawn

A delicate line to be drawn

Between brain and brawn

To not cometh between too far

All that we are

And to the outer yet reach next

Between heaven and what is vexed

To not cometh between

To not there render unseen

And to the inner most side

Between love and pride

To not deal in death yet as desist are

To be a living star

Living and loving life giving

We all can be as are

Girl Dress -
Black Kissed One (two) & Three

What was it as I am nigh here nigh high ten?

Home When

Goal to new castle then

Obviously when

The woman just had come as

Too two well

She had me there knowing

Was mad as back black hell well

The whole system stank

As three dwell

The women woman was rank rest cowing

Blacking

Me to black dress

Kissed as standing

Now and same

What wonder eh ginning?

Door-a fridge-cracking

The sound of living light

Right sighting me fight

Writing'

Wedding

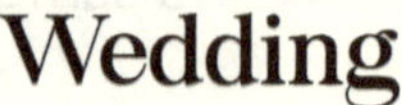

A woman of pearly white

A woman of gold

A woman dressed black be

With a....A madman down black

A monk of white

With gold carrying he

With a.... A promise of this

A promise of that

And forever we

& u wer

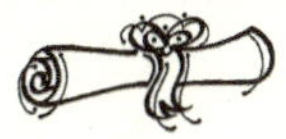

To yew for and

Hold my Hand to you

Cover shirt feel

See the armour

God and gift

To yew

Hew

Find

For there be 4 written for

Madness appears

I am not why

Messaging works

And then does die

Freedom to roam

Does not exist

Cannot allowed to myself get pissed

Children slower to reply

Brother aborted me to while away the day

And hour

Where my only lonely be live

Here writing stuff to the stars

What is as if life a truck-load?

Of science and art

Just allow suffer her to me

I sit alas man bended knee

Will alone if not married

Be as we

Told by PC that is her open

And yet free

Can forgive and remember prior

Give her my hand and desire

Please her God and her be

Fuel my ample feeling see

What is man to twist

Unshackled thought

A woman truthful this I

Perceive

Am real do nought deceive

Grant me certain wiles

From the

Likes of men

This is surely the grant of heaven

Peace to War

A pacifist desire is not wrong

Love does more herald this song

The hardness of life

To live all long

Future need and self-belong

God be I know not wrong

Money and wellness not to avoid

The shackled aisle of

To avoid poverty fear

Give and fear not so be

Live to remain more of life

And the fuel of life

And the sounding black and white more wisely

Yet not Solomon's grasping hand

Yet see to it cut a man or

Woman down by sword will

Never from warlike.....no

Not...........simply further

Poverty

And go against

Goodness and posterity

Thence PO

C'est Fini

(After Edward De Bono)

Mental Illness

Mental illness is like the war of the mind

With vagaries of subsistence

And sleeping not usual

Amid the shootings of zebra

A kindly mind to itself and mostly

Wanting to be found

And leaving aside all else

Will be a-giving

It that encompasses around

And all there is to a love

Looking and comfort kiss

Clasping and judgment proper sought

Yet thirsts and hungers

For all there the thought

And physical torture

To love what the heck said

The Bride

It's the coming of the bride

And the happening inside

It's the breaking in two

Of the stick we once knew

It's the hammer-fist duke

There I contemplate to puke

What is then to be

Said the birds to the bee